THE TOTTENHAM JOINT LINES

A PHOTOGRAPHIC JOURNEY
Between
BARKING and GOSPEL OAK

By J.E. Connor

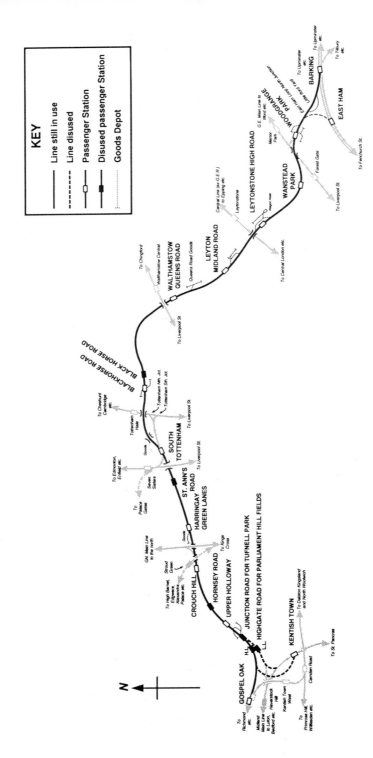

THE BARKING - GOSPEL OAK ROUTE and ASSOCIATED LINES

KEY

———— Line still in use

- - - - Line disused

Passenger Station

Disused passenger Station

Goods Depot

CONTENTS

Dedicated to the memory of my father,

J.P. Connor

1920 - 1993.

*A former employee of the L.N.E.R. and B.R., without whose
encouragement I would probably have never taken an interest in the history of
my native East End, and the railways of London in general.*

ISBN 0 947699 20 1
Copyright Connor & Butler 1993
Typesetting : Connor & Butler
Cover Design and General Layout : J.E. Connor
Route Map : P.B. Butler
Proofs Checked by P.A.J. Perris
Printed by The Owl Printing Co., Tollesbury Essex.

This is the first in my series of photographic journeys around some of London's most interesting railway routes.

The books are intended as a pictorial record, and although they do not pretend to be complete histories, they will of course include all the main facts about the lines concerned. For those requiring further information, a select bibliography has been included for reference, although it is only fair to mention that some of the works listed are long out of print, and consequently difficult to find.

My acquaintance with the Tottenham & Forest Gate and Tottenham & Hampstead Joint Lines really started in the mid-1960's, when a newly acquired job with British Rail provided me with both the necessary funds, and a staff identity card which allowed me quarter-price travel.

With this trusty green card, and a roll or two of Agfa CT18, I sallied forth at weekends exploring the capital's rail network, and discovering its many attractions.

My interest has always been in the entire Greater London area, but as a native East Ender, I suppose I was inclined to favour my own district. and because of this, one of the first routes to catch my attention was that from Barking to Kentish Town.

My initial visit took me to Wanstead Park, and I fell in love with the station immediately. Although clearly of Midland parentage, the buildings were painted in the green and cream colours of the Eastern Region. The reason for this being that in 1949, not long after Nationalisation, the section of line between Barking and Harringay Park was transferred from the London Midland Region to the Eastern, and that the stations were painted accordingly. From a point west of Harringay however, the route remained LM, and the stations appeared in maroon and cream. The regional difference also showed on the nameboards, which were dark blue for the Eastern, and maroon for the Midland.

At most of the stations, gaslighting was still the norm, and many of the dimly lit, but wonderfully atmospheric booking offices, still retained a few old Pre-Nationalisation tickets in their racks. Some of these displayed former names, such as Leyton without the 'Midland Road', and Leytonstone without the 'High Road', and of course these seemed very exciting to a youngster just starting to develop an interest in collecting tickets.

Most of the little goods depots along the route were still functioning at this time, and I regret not photographing them. However, my chief passion was for passenger stations, so I concentrated almost entirely on these.

Disused stations often have a fascination for many, and this line could boast a handful. Unfortunately most had been largely demolished by the 1960's, although bits of derelict platforms remained, as did the odd street level building.

One rather strange incident that I recall was when a well dressed middle aged lady approached a friend and myself near Seven Sisters, and asked directions to St. Ann's Road station. Apparently a male acquaintance had made a date with her, and suggested that they met by the entrance. Sadly he failed to tell her that it had been shut since the Second World War! I wonder if they managed to meet up eventually!

I also regret that I never knew the line in steam days, although I remember changing from the Underground to BR at Barking once, and seeing a grubby Fowler 4F 0-6-0 pass through with a St. Pancras - Tilbury boat train. This had obviously travelled over the route, as did many similar workings, but unfortunately this was well before I knew how to handle a camera.

Before dieselisation, the local passenger services were usually worked by Stanier or Fowler 2-6-2 tanks, whilst freight trains brought a mixture of motive power ranging from various ex LMS and LNER types, through to the occasional Bulleid Q1 0-6-0 from the Southern.

All this variety, together with the differences in station paint schemes retained the 'joint line' atmosphere well after Nationalisation. However, like so many things, it was too good to last, and eventually it changed completely. First steam disappeared, then the goods yards closed, and finally the distinctive station buildings were demolished, and replaced in most cases by little spartan brick huts. Semaphore signalling is now restricted to the area around Harringay, and no doubt this will be replaced by colour lights in due course.

Early in 1981, the local passenger workings were diverted to serve Gospel Oak instead of Kentish Town, and the connection previously used at the western end was severed and dismantled. At the time of writing, just a few of the station booking offices remain open, and these are generally staffed during the morning peak periods only. Otherwise tickets have to be obtained from a conductor guard on the train.

It is hoped that this little book will serve as a reminder to those who knew the line as it once was, and also as a source of reference to those who are only familiar with the route in its present form

J.E. Connor
1993

G. E. R.

41400

Hornsey Road

G. E. R.

Junction Road

G. E. R.

Highgate Road

A selection of G.E.R. luggage labels.

J.E. Connor

It doesn't seem long ago that the route taken by the present Barking - Gospel Oak service still abounded with visible reminders of its pre-grouping origins. However, a lot of these disappeared when facilities were rationalised in the 1970's, and an air of dereliction began to set in. Nevertheless, for the railway minded, a journey along the line remains fascinating, and a great deal of historic interest can still be seen.

Barking station is situated seven and a half miles from Fenchurch Street, and is currently served by both British Rail and London Underground trains.

It was one of the original stopping places on the London, Tilbury & Southend Railway, and was opened along with the initial stretch of line between Forest Gate Junction and Tilbury on 13th April, 1854.

As built, the premises were very basic, but large enough to deal with the anticipated traffic. The entrance was situated to the south of the line, on the London side of East Street level crossing, and adjoining this could be found the Station Master's house. It was very countrified in appearance, but then in 1854, Barking itself was still only a fishing village. However, urbanisation quickly followed in the railway's wake, and it eventually became necessary to make alterations.

An up side bay was opened in 1889, and at the same time, the down platform was rebuilt as an island, therefore providing a loop. These improvements were to prove invaluable as traffic increased. On 9th July 1894, the Tottenham & Forest Gate Railway was opened, and this allowed the Midland direct access to LTSR metals. The following year saw the introduction of through workings between St.Pancras and Southend, all of which, of course, travelled via Barking.

Nevertheless the premises sufficed until the early years of the Twentieth Century, when the Metropolitan District Railway extended their services into the station, by way of the Whitechapel & Bow line, which was opened on 2nd June 1902. By this time, Barking, although still technically in Essex, was fast becoming a part of Greater London, and the simple country station could no longer cope with its new role.

To accommodate the extra traffic, the LTSR obtained powers in 1902 to quadruple their lines between Campbell Road Junction, Bow, and Barking, and work began on this immediately. The tracks to East Ham were completed in 1905, but the section east of here was delayed whilst additional land was acquired and substantial rebuilding took place.

The old East Street level crossing disappeared in 1906, and was replaced by a road overbridge. On the west side of this bridge, the new street level building arose. It was much larger than its predecessor, and although fairly plain in appearance, was not unattractive. The frontage was largely constructed of yellow stock bricks, and featured a symmetrical pair of Dutch gables. There were doorways at each end, separated by a row of five windows, and these were topped by shallow segmental arches of red brick. The remainder of the structure however, was weatherboarded and purely functional, although both ends included some nice Venetian style windows.

At track level, four islands were constructed, providing the station with eight platform faces, all of which were furnished with substantial buildings and awnings.

Rebuilding was complete by 1908, and the little country station had been totally transformed.

For a while, the surrounding district seems to have retained an air of suburban gentility, and as such, provided the subject for a music hall song entitled ' Pretty Little Villa Down At Barking '. This was sung in typically acidic tones by that doyen of Cockney artistes, Gus Elen, and told of a family who moved from a wooden slum in Peckham to one of the smart new houses then being built on the London outskirts. As with the majority of Elen's songs it was full of sarcastic humour, but it gives us an idea how the area was viewed during the Edwardian era. The chorus went like this:-

> *"So come dahn,*
> *An' 'ear the sparrers sing.*
> *In the middle a' the winter,*
> *Yer would fancy it was spring.*
> *The missus an' the kids*
> *Are gettin' brahn as anyfing.*
> *Oh come dahn an' see us all at Barkin'."*

Barking station remained virtually unchanged for the next fifty years, although the tracks to the east were quadrupled when the District Line services were extended to Upminster in 1932. Further rebuilding however was deemed necessary during the late 1950's when preparations were being made for the LTS Line electrification.

The work included substantial track alterations in shape of new flyovers and dive-unders to improve traffic flow, although the number of platforms remained the same. Nevertheless, a great deal of demolition was required and for a while towards the end of 1958, a temporary wooden bay platform was provided on the north side of the formation for trains serving Kentish Town.

The job of rebuilding took five years, and was finally completed in September 1961. By this time, the old street level building had been swept away and replaced by an uninspiring edifice comprising a great deal of concrete and glass.

The Fenchurch Street services were fully electrified in June 1962, and the steam hauled trains of yesteryear became just a memory.

The present day service to Gospel Oak normally departs from Platform One, and is generally formed of a two car DMU.

On leaving Barking, the train negotiates a flyover, before reaching a bridge which carries it over the River Roding. Beyond here, the tracks pass beneath the A406, and the Fenchurch Street main line can be seen diverging to the south. This was opened by the LTSR on 31st March 1858, and provided a more convenient means of reach-

Above: A general view of Barking station in the 1930's, with LMSR Stanier 2-6-4T No.2534 on an up working to Fenchurch Street, and a District Line 'F' Stock train bound for Hounslow.
Author's Collection

Below: Fowler Class 3MT 2-6-2T No.40029 of Kentish Town MPD approaches the bay platform at East Ham with a train off the Tottenham & Hampstead line, early in 1958.
B. Pask

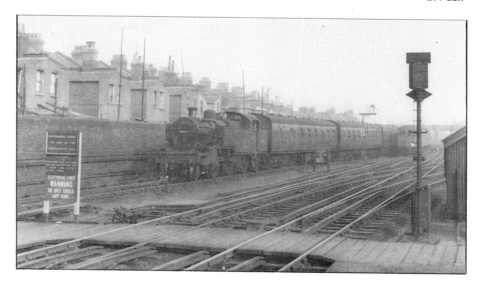

ing the City than the original route through Forest Gate and Stratford. Just beyond the Junction are situated the car sheds built for the electrification of 1962.

Our Gospel Oak train continues to Little Ilford, where the site of the disused East Ham curve trails in on the up side. This line was opened by the LTS on 9th July 1894, at the same time as the Tottenham and Forest Gate Railway, and provided a link from the Midland to East Ham. When East Ham station was rebuilt in 1904 - 5, a bay platform for these trains was constructed to the north of the premises, and this continued in use until the spur closed to passengers on 15th September 1958. The line officially stayed open for freight for a few more weeks until 30th November, although it was little used and soon abandoned. The course of the spur ran to the east of Shakespeare Crescent, and its site, although still definable in places, has been largely redeveloped.

The first station out of Barking is situated at Woodgrange Park. This was also opened by the LTSR on 9th July 1894, and has its entrance on the east side of Romford Road. From here, covered stairways lead down to track level, where two side platforms and a dock were provided. The buildings were of red brick, but these were demolished in the 1970's and only a fragment on the down side still remains.

An adjacent goods yard was opened to the south of the station in the autumn of 1894, but this was closed on 7th December 1964, and has since been replaced by new housing.

The down side stairway at Woodgrange Park in 1972, showing a directional sign which listed the abandoned route to East Ham amongst its destinations.

I. Baker

Above: Woodgrange Park station, looking towards Kentish Town from the up side in 1968.

Below : Woodgrange Park, as seen from the down side in 1972.

Both J.E. Connor

The dock has also been long devoid of track, and the premises currently present a somewhat sorry sight. However, the signal box, which is situated at the east end of the down platform, remains in use, and continues to provide a point of interest, albeit now fitted with somewhat incongruous modern windows.

Well into the 1970's a blue enamel sign survived at the top of the down stairway directing passengers to both Barking and East Ham. No attempt had been made to blank out the latter, despite there being no trains since 1958!

The original street level accommodation largely disappeared some years ago, when a new booking office was constructed. However, a small section still survives which consists of a single bricked-up doorway.

Beyond Woodgrange Park we leave the former LTSR, which diverges on the down side and leads to Forest Gate Junction where it joins the ex Great Eastern main line. Although this section lost its ordinary passenger trains from 1st May 1918, a very limited late night service has operated since 1968 providing a link between Liverpool Street and Barking.

From Woodgrange Park Junction we are on Tottenham & Forest Gate Railway metals, and we climb up to cross the Great Eastern before proceeding to the next station which is at Wanstead Park.

The Tottenham & Forest Gate Railway was jointly promoted by the Midland and LTSR, and was constructed following an Act of Parliament passed on 4th August 1890. From its opening four years later, the Midland operated a local service from either Moorgate or St Pancras to East Ham, and in 1895, as previously mentioned, four daily through workings were introduced between St. Pancras and Southend. These were joined from 1st May 1896, by boat trains linking St. Pancras with Tilbury, which continued to run until the LTS line was electrified.

The line was to prove strategically useful, particularly when the Midland reached a provisional agreement to take over the operating of the LTS in 1911. Despite numerous objections from the Great Eastern, who also had their eyes on the Tilbury system, the Midland's bill received Royal Assent on 7th August 1912, and the LTSR, as a company ceased to exist.

Wanstead Park station has its entrance off the east side of Woodgrange Road, and opened with the line in 1894.

The viaduct was widened to accommodate the platforms, and a large booking hall was provided in one of the arches below. The platform buildings were constructed of wood, and clearly owed their architectural origins to the Midland. They were situated about half way along the station's length, and were bracketed out from the viaduct sides. Two covered stairways led from the booking hall, and surfaced at the opposite end of the platform buildings.

The delightful station in its green and cream paintwork was the first on the line to be rationalised, and it fell to the demolition men in 1970.

Above: Wanstead Park looking west in February 1969.

Below: Wanstead Park looking east in February 1969.

Both J.E. Connor

13

The booking office was replaced by a portakabin, and tickets continued to be issued until a fire in the late 1980's, after which the station was de-staffed.

The little signalbox which once stood at the west end of the up platform has also been obliterated, and in common with other stations on the line, Wanstead Park now appears gaunt and desolate. The once lavish double stairways on either side have been reduced to half their former width, leaving the remaining section minus stairs and derelict. Down below, around the burnt out arches which once housed the booking office, a few reminders of the past just about survive, albeit somewhat obscure. Large wooden barrier gates remain in-situ, although long since out of use. Those leading to the down side are still painted in the old familiar shade of green, which has now faded to something resembling a matt finish turquoise. The same colour can also be found in minute quantities elsewhere on the premises, where insignificant fragments of the former structure escaped the attentions of the demolition men. The current platform shelters comprise a matching pair of brick huts, both of which contain sections of vintage bench seating, which were presumably salvaged from the original buildings.

Abundant ragwort, growing through cracks in the platform, and alongside the track, completes the sad picture of dereliction.

From here, the line continues on viaduct until it reaches the next station which is at Leytonstone High Road.

Opened as Leytonstone in 1894, the structure was very similar in appearance to Wanstead Park, with two side platforms and wooden buildings. This time however, only those on the up side were bracketed out from the viaduct, as the formation was built wide enough to accommodate a double track loop behind the down platform. The reason for this was to serve a street level goods depot which ran alongside the north face of the viaduct. Because of its close proximity to the GE Epping line, there was not enough space to provide a headshunt, and therefore a hydraulic wagon hoist had to be installed.

The existence of all this meant that the stairway leading to the down platform was built into the viaduct, and not constructed externally as on the other side.

The station was re-named Leytonstone High Road on 1st May 1949. and rebuilt in the late 1950's following fire damage.

In turn, the new buildings have also been partially burnt, and badly vandalised. Like Wanstead Park, the booking office has been removed, and the station has been reduced to the status of an un-staffed halt.

The goods yard closed on 6th May 1968, and has since disappeared, although a widening of the viaduct indicates the site of the loop.

At the time of writing, the signalbox remains at the west end, still displaying its name as Leytonstone, without any reference to the High Road suffix. However with its semaphores now replaced by colour lights, its survival will no doubt be short lived.

Leytronstone High Road : A rare view of the platforms before the station was rebuilt.
Lens of Sutton

Soon after departing from the station, our train passes over the ex-Great Eastern line from Stratford to Epping, and a glance down will no doubt be rewarded by the sight of a Central Line train rattling underneath.

The viaduct continues in a north-westerly direction, and passes the side of the disused Leyton Goods & Coal Depot, before reaching Leyton Midland Road.

Architecturally, this station was another in the Midland mould, and was very similar to both Wanstead Park and Leytonstone.

The entrance is on the east side of Leyton High Road, and originally comprised of a glazed wooden structure built around an arch which accommodated the booking office. From here, covered stairways ascended either side of the viaduct to reach the platforms. The wooden buildings were again bracketed onto the viaduct, and those on the down side were directly above the pavement of Midland Road which runs parallel to the line.

A signalbox at the Barking end controlled the goods yard and associated sidings, but this has long disappeared. The yard itself closed in 1968, and has now been redeveloped as an industrial estate. The more observant traveller may notice a grassy section of embankment on the down side which was once used for a headshunt.

Above: Leytonstone High Road looking west in March 1993, showing the late 1950's buildings, vandalised and boarded up.

Below: Leytonstone High Road signalbox, also in March 1993.

Both C.D.J. Connor

Leyton Midland Road, looking west on a gloomy February afternoon in 1966.

J.E. Connor

The passenger station was renamed Leyton Midland Road on 1st May 1949, and lost its buildings to rationalisation in 1971.

The line remains on a north-westerly course, en-route to Walthamstow. For a short distance it is still on viaduct, but before the next station it descends into cutting. The viaduct itself, which stretches back to beyond Wanstead Park is quite extensive, and comprises 386 arches.

On the down side we pass the redeveloped site of Queens Road Goods and Coal Depot, again opened in 1894 and closed on 6th May 1968. In this day and age it seems strange to imagine all these small establishments functioning, but before the onset of the current fad for motor lorries, such places were vital to the local economy. Judging from the crowded conditions on the roads, it seems a terrible pity that they were ever abandoned.

Walthamstow passenger station is tucked away from the main thoroughfares on the east side of Edinburgh Road. It has a neat brick street level building from which a glazed and roofed footbridge once led above the tracks and reached the platforms by means of covered stairways. The platform buildings were again constructed of wood, and were similar to the other TFGR stations previously described.

At one time, there was a signalbox at the east end of the down platform, but this

Above: Walthamstow station, looking towards Barking in 1966.

Below: Walthamstow, by now suffixed 'Queens Road', looking towards Kentish Town in 1969.
Both J.E. Connor

18

Above: The street level building at Walthamstow in 1968.

J.E. Connor

Below: The down platform at Walthamstow Queens Road, as viewed from a train in 1972. The station is in the initial stages of demolition, with the covering removed from the footbridge.

I. Baker

was abolished in pre-grouping days.

The wooden buildings with their characteristic awnings disappeared towards the end of 1972, and the platforms are now somewhat overgrown. During rationalisation, gaslighting was also changed to electric, the stairways were rebuilt, and the canopy above the station entrance was removed.

It was renamed Walthamstow Queen's Road on 6th May 1968, although this seems rather odd, as the premises are a fair distance from Queen's Road itself.

Recently, a short flight of unlit steps has been added at the north end of the down platform, which crosses a piece of derelict land, and eventually leads to the upside entrance of Walthamstow Central. The stations are only about 200 yards apart by this route, and the footpath is intended to provide an interchange.

Walthamstow Queens Road : Nameboards in transition, 1969.

J.E. Connor

Beyond Walthamstow Queens Road, the line passes beneath the former GE Chingford branch, and continues in cutting to the site of the original station at Black Horse Road.

Again opened with the line in 1894, Black Horse Road was provided with a street level building very similar to the one at Walthamstow. This led to a covered footbridge, from which enclosed ramps descended to the platforms. These were provided with typical TFGR wooden buildings, and were lit by gas. Originally, the lamp posts, which were of a standard Midland Railway design, were fitted with square lamp cases, but these were later changed to LMS glass bowls with Sugg 'Rochester' suspended mantles.

These survived until the early 1970's, when they were replaced by temporary electric lighting, during the preliminary stages of modernisation. Shortly afterwards, the wooden buildings were knocked down and replaced by basic uninviting brick shelters.

Stanier Class 3MT 2-6-2T No.40111 stands wreathed in steam at Black Horse Road station with a train for Barking in January 1960. At this time the locomotive was allocated to Kentish Town MPD.

T. Wright

Prior to Nationalisation, the station's name always appears to have been displayed as Black Horse Road, but from the 1950's onwards *Blackhorse* was sometimes shown as a single word. This rather confusing inconsistency was largely confined to nameboards, although it occasionally occurred on tickets as well. The nearby LT Underground station, which opened in 1968, was named Blackhorse Road from the start, but the official designation of the BR premises still seemed to remain uncertain. The large enamel sign above the street level entrance displayed *Black Horse* as two separate words, as did one of the platform running-in boards, but the lamp post totems exhibited the other version. However, when these were replaced in the

Above: The street level building at Black Horse Road station in 1970.

Below: General view of Black Horse Road, looking from the footbridge towards Barking.

Both J.E. Connor

Above: The west end of Black Horse Road looking towards Kentish Town in 1971.
The present station is situated on the other side of the road overbridge.
Below: A view from the up platform at Black Horse Road looking towards
Kentish Town in 1970.

Both J.E. Connor

1970's by British Rail corporate image signs, the first part of the title reverted to its original form.

For those who appreciate such things, Black Horse Road, in common with the other original stations on the TFGR, was a pure delight. Even a quarter of a century ago, its fading green and cream paintwork, gaslamps, and dark blue totems, made it seem like something out of the past. Not long before the structure's demise, a specialist model railway manufacturer marketed some Midland Railway canopy valencing, which was stated on the packaging to be based on the prototype at Black Horse Road. Surely this must be the first, and so far the only time, that an east London station has been commemorated in this way!

Black Horse Road was resited to the opposite side of the bridge on 14th December 1981, to afford better interchange with the LT Victoria Line. Virtually all traces of the old station have now disappeared, although fragments of broken platform are still vaguely visible beneath the trackside foliage.

The new station, which incidentally displays the *Blackhorse* part of its title as a single word, is reached through the LT booking hall. The current platforms occupy the site of some sidings which served an adjacent goods depot until its closure on 7th December 1964. Black Horse Road signalbox stood to the north of the formation, and there was once a single track, carried on a level crossing into a factory estate on the far side of Forest Road.

Fairburn 2-6-4T No.42237 approaches Black Horse Road in the late 1950's

B. Pask

The TFGR continues westwards, skirting reservoirs on either side, before passing over the Great Eastern Lea Valley Line, and joining with the Tottenham & Hampstead Railway at South Tottenham Junction. A Midland goods and coal depot, reached from THJ metals, functioned to the north of the formation from 1st May 1871 until 4th July 1966, but this has now disappeared.

The Tottenham & Hampstead Junction Railway came into being following an Act of 28th July 1862, and eventually stretched from Tottenham North Junction on the Great Eastern, to Gospel Oak, where trains terminated at a single platform adjoining the North London Line station of the same name.

The first section was opened from Tottenham to Highgate Road on 21st July 1868, and was initially served by GE trains from Fenchurch Street. These travelled via Stratford, and had to reverse at Tottenham station. This rather complicated routing was to prove unpopular, and the service was withdrawn early in 1870. Later that year, the Midland opened a curve between Highgate Road and Kentish Town, but due to financial problems, the THJR's own line to Gospel Oak was not completed until 1888.

The route proved to be a useful link between the Midland and Great Eastern, and provided a means by which the two companies could enjoy running powers over certain sections of each other's lines. Midland freight workings now had direct access to the docks, without having to pay the heavy tolls levied by the North London Railway, and the GE could operate into St.Pancras.

From 1st July 1902, the THJR came under the joint management of both these companies, and its title was changed to the Tottenham & Hampstead Joint Committee.

South Tottenham station was added on 1st May 1871, and was furnished with a small booking office on the east side of Tottenham High Road. From here, ramps led up to two wooden platforms which were constructed on the top of the embankment. Before demolition and rebuilding in the 1970's, there was a weather-boarded waiting shelter on the up side, and a red brick counterpart opposite. Judging from its appearance this seems to have been a later addition, although the wooden building was probably original.

From opening until 1949, the station's official title was South Tottenham & Stamford Hill.

The old wooden platforms have been replaced by concrete, but the booking office survives, as does the signalbox at the east end of the up side.

Immediately to the west of the station can be seen South Tottenham Junction, where a sharply curving spur to Seven Sisters on the GE Edmonton and Enfield line climbs northwards on a gradient of 1-in-110. This was opened to goods traffic during 1879, and then to passengers on 1st January 1880. Since the withdrawal of the North Woolwich - Palace Gates service on 7th January 1963, there have been no regular passenger trains, and the former double track has now been singled.

Above: The present Blackhorse Road station, looking west in March 1993.

C.D.J. Connor

Below: The exterior of South Tottenham in 1973.
At the time of writing, the building still survives and is little changed.

J.E. Connor

Above: South Tottenham looking east from the up platform in 1967.

Below: South Tottenham looking east in 1967, but this time from the down side.

Both J.E. Connor

Fowler 3MT 2-6-2T No.40034, fitted with condensing apparatus, draws to a stand
at South Tottenham station with a Kentish Town - Barking train in April 1959.

T. Wright

MIDLAND RAILWAY.—Between Tottenham, St. Pancras, Ludgate Hill, Moorgate Street, &c.

⁎⁎ The Time Table not having arrived at the time of going to press, the Publisher cannot vouch for the correctness of these times.

DOWN TRAINS.	WEEK DAYS.	SUNDAYS.
Moorgate Street...... dep.		
Aldersgate Street ... ,,		
Ludgate Hill .... ,,		
Farringdon Street... ,,		
King's Cross (Met.) ,,		
St. Pancras ...... ,,		
Camden Road .... ,, arr.		
Kentish Town... { dep.		
Highgate Road		
Upper Holloway		
Crouch Hill		
South Tottenham . . . arr.		

UP TRAINS.	WEEK DAYS.	SUNDAYS.
South Tottenham...dep.		
Crouch Hill		
Upper Holloway		
Highgate Road .... arr.		
Kentish Town... { dep.		
Camden Road .... arr.		
St. Pancras .... ,,		
King's Cross (Met.) ,,		
Farringdon Street... ,,		
Ludgate Hill .... ,,		
Aldersgate Street ... ,,		
Moorgate Street... ,,		

A.—Passengers to or from Ludgate Hill and L. C. and D Line, by Trains marked A, do not change Carriages ; by other Trains they change at Farringdon Street.
B.—Passengers from Moorgate Street for Tottenham and Hampstead Line, by Trains marked B, change Carriage at Kentish Town.
C.—Passengers from St. Pancras for Tottenham and Hampstead Line, by Trains marked C, change Carriages at Kentish Town.
D.—Passengers from Tottenham and Hampstead Line for Moorgate Street, by Trains marked D, change Carriages at Kentish Town.
E.—Passengers from Tottenham and Hampstead Line for St. Pancras, by Trains marked E, change Carriages at Kentish Town.

Midland timetable for May 1871, showing trains serving the newly opened station at South Tottenham

28

Beyond here, our train travels beneath the Enfield line, then passes the earthworks of an unfinished spur from the GE which trails in on the up side. This was partially constructed in Pre-Grouping days, but abandoned before completion. Shortly after this, we reach the site of St.Ann's Road station.

St.Ann's Road was one of three unremunerative stations which closed during the Second World War.

It was opened on 2nd October 1882, apparently with a great deal of celebration. This is how the event was recorded in the Tottenham & Edmonton Weekly Herald for Friday 6th October 1882:-

"On Monday morning last the new station on the Tottenham & Hampstead Junction Railway erected for the accommodation of the large and increasing districts of St.Ann's was opened for public traffic. Originally it was intended that the opening should take place on 1st June last, but unavoidable delays prevented the arrangement being carried out. All the trains from South Tottenham to Moorgate Street will now stop at the new station which will be a boon to the neighbourhood as hitherto travellers from St. Ann's Road had to go either to Stamford Hill or Seven Sisters station on the GE system. The opening was regarded with great satisfaction in the locality. Flags of all nations supplied by messrs. Eveniss and Pike, proprietors of the Victoria Tavern, St.Ann's Road, were suspended from one side of the road to the other, and various tradesmen met to congratulate themselves upon the long deferred benefit having come at last. There is no doubt whatever that the new station will largely add to the prosperity of St.Ann's district, by bringing to it a considerable number of additional residents, the want of proper railway accommodation having hitherto been a great drawback. On Monday evening there was a brilliant display of fireworks from an elevated position of the Victoria Tavern. A large crowd assembled, but everything passed off without a hitch of any kind."

The street level building was a small red brick affair, positioned on the west side of Seven Sisters Road, close to the junction with St. Ann's Road. Ramps and steps led from here to two wooden platforms which were cantilevered at the top of the embankment, and a signalbox was situated slightly east of the station on the down side. Wooden waiting shelters were provided on each platform, both of which had slate roofs and timber valencing.

St. Ann's Road closed on 9th August 1942, and being constructed almost entirely of wood, soon fell into a state of disrepair. The closure was described by G.H.Lake in his classic volume 'The Railways of Tottenham':-

"...The booking office doors just closed for the last time and next day a disinterested public passed by quite oblivious of the fact that almost exactly sixty years earlier those same doors had opened to the accompaniment of fireworks."

The platforms and associate structures were removed sometime in the late 1940's, but the street level building survived, and is now used as a shop.

Above*:* The exterior of St. Ann's Road station, as it appeared in the early years of the present century.

Commercial postcard. Alan A. Jackson Collection

Below*:* An LMS Fowler class 4F 0-6-0 rattles past the disused platforms at St. Ann's Road, sometime in the late 1940's.

G. Weller Collection

Until comparatively recent times the decapitated remains of a lamp post could be seen alongside the ramp which once led to the up platform, and this may possibly still be in-situ. However, with the growth of foliage alongside the embankment, it's very difficult to see whether it's there or not, particularly with the brief glimpse that's obtainable from a passing train.

Having passed the site of St. Ann's Road, we continue on embankment to the much re-named THJ station at Harringay.

This was opened with the title Green Lanes on 1st June 1880, and changed to Harringay Park, Green Lanes three years later. The suffix

St. Ann's Road signalbox c1948.
G. Weller Collection

was dropped, leaving it simply as 'Harringay Park' on 18th June 1951, only to be completely changed again on 27th October 1958 to Harringay Stadium. With the demise of the nearby dog track it became Harringay East on 12th May 1990, but this was obviously deemed unsuitable as just over a year later, on 8th July 1991, it received the name Harringay Green Lanes. The title therefore having turned almost full circle.

The little red brick booking office is situated off the east side of Green Lanes, and is connected to the platforms by ramps, in a similar manner to both South Tottenham and St. Ann's Road. The structure appears to be original, although it is not shown on a 25" OS plan of 1896. However, it is indicated quite clearly on a similar map published nineteen years later, therefore indicating that it might have been a later addition. The old wooden platform buildings were swept away when the station was rebuilt in the 1950's, and replaced by modern structures. Of these, only the

31

Above: The street level building at St. Ann's Road in 1978.

J.E. Connor

Below: Harringay Green Lanes station, looking west in March 1993.

C.D.J. Connor

Above: Crouch Hill exterior in May 1966. The street level building still survives, and has changed little over the years.

Below: Crouch Hill looking west in May 1966.

Both J.E. Connor

former shelter on the down side survives, albeit boarded up and derelict. Near the east end of the opposite platform, a disused stairway dating from the rebuilding, once gave access to the now vanished stadium, a relic of the days when "A night at the dogs" was a popular London recreation.

Today's passengers have to make do with new brick waiting shelters, which have been erected at the entrance end of the platforms. No doubt they are functional, but they could scarcely be called attractive, despite their brightly painted red roofs.

To the west of the station. a goods yard existed on the down side from 1st June 1880, until 3rd February 1964, but this has now disappeared beneath a jungle of bushes.

From here, the route descends into cutting and passes under the Great Northern Main line, before reaching Harringay Park Junction, where a single track spur from the GN trails in on the down side. It was originally intended to construct this connection in the 1880's, and some track was laid at the THJ end. However the junction with the Great Northern remained unbuilt, and the rails were lifted in 1885. The formation then remained dormant until the first World War, when track was reinstated, and the line finally brought into use on 15th May 1916. With the end of the emergency it became surplus to requirements and closed in 1920. However, when hostilities broke out again, it was hastily brought back into commission and re-opened on 8th January 1940. Apart from the obvious wartime uses of troop and munition movements, it has proved a worthwhile connection, and it still exists, although it has never seen regular passenger traffic.

Beyond this junction, the route continues in a south-westerly direction, and passes through a short tunnel beneath the disused GN Northern Heights branch which crosses the route immediately west of Hall Road. This line finally closed to passengers on 5th July 1954, and until demolition following fire damage in 1966, THJ passengers could look up and catch a glimpse of the abandoned Stroud Green station high on its viaduct. The section of trackbed between Finsbury Park and Highgate, including the site of Stroud Green, is now used as a public footpath.

Next we come to the platforms at Crouch Hill, which are sparse and empty, apart from a pair of 1970's brick shelters.

This station was opened on 21st July 1868, and served by the initial G.E. trains between Fenchurch Street and Highgate Road. When these ceased at the end of January 1870, the premises closed, but they reopened a few months later, to be used by a Midland service originating at Moorgate Street. Crouch Hill has remained open ever since, and although the antiquated platform awnings disappeared in the late 1960's the station house still survives, as does the adjoining street level building. Inside here, the ticket office retains its wooden panelled screen, and apart from being painted white, this appears to be more or less original.

For lovers of Victoriana, a short distance to the left of the station entrance can be found the facade of the Friern Manor Dairy Farm, with its decorative panels illustrating how milk was once brought from the cow to the home.

Continuing south west from Crouch Hill, the train remains in cutting, and soon passes the site of Hornsey Road, another of the line's stations abandoned in the Second World War.

It opened on 1st January 1872, and had its entrance on the western side of the road after which it was named. It consisted of two platforms, seemingly with wooden buildings similar to those at St. Ann's Road and Harringay, and had a small brick booking office at street level. Demolition appears to have taken place relatively soon after closure on 3rd May 1943, as a photograph taken eight years later shows it with platforms only. These survived in a derelict overgrown state for some years, but have now gone, and the site is virtually undiscernable.

LTSR 4-4-2T, No.39 *'Forest Gate'* passes Hornsey Road with a through train to Southend around the turn of the century.

The LTSR named their locomotives after stations and districts that they served, including some on the TFGR and the THJR. Amongst these were *'Leyton'* (No.32), *'Wanstead'* (No.33), *'Tottenham'* (No.34), *'Walthamstow'* (No.36), *'Woodgrange'* (No.37), *'Forest Gate'* (No.39), *'Black Horse Road'* (No.40), *'Leytonstone'* (No.41), *'Little Ilford'* (No.48), *'Harringay'* (No.56), *'Crouch Hill'* (No.57), *'Hornsey Road'* (No.58), *'Holloway'* (No.59), *'Highgate Road'* (No.60), and *'Kentish Town'* (No.61). All of these were 4-4-2Ts.

No.40, *'Black Horse Road'* exchanged names with No. 13, *'Benfleet'* in 1911 .

Author's Collection

Above: Midland Railway 2-4-0, No.1081, on a short St. Pancras - Southend train, passes a Midland 0-4-4T running light at Hornsey Road around the turn of the century.

D. Brennand Collection

Below: A Stanier 3MT 2-6-2T stands at Upper Holloway station with a Barking - Kentish Town train in January 1960. The LMSR 'Hawkseye' style nameboards add to the period charm

T. Wright.

Past the site of Hornsey Road, the train rumbles beneath Holloway Road and pauses at Upper Holloway Station.

This opened on 21st July 1868, and suffered the same short period of early closure as Crouch Hill. The distinctive platform awnings with curved corrugated iron tops survived in the late 1960's, as did the former LMSR 'Hawkseye' nameboards. Curiously it seems that Crouch Hill was never equipped with totem signs, and was therefore unique in being the only station on the line, open in BR days, not so treated.

The small brick street level building still stands, and adjoins the footbridge which leads to the platforms.

Upper Holloway station looking east, late on a murky January afternoon in 1966.
J.E. Connor

Beyond Upper Holloway, the line passes the site of the once extensive Tufnell Park Goods Depot, opened by the Great Eastern in 1886 largely to serve the Metropolitan Cattle Market. Cattle pens and other necessary facilities were provided, and the depot was very busy on market days. On arrival, the trains would unload, and the animals would then be driven on foot along Tufnell Park Road to their destination at Caledonian Road. With the increase of road haulage the premises fell into decline, and they closed on 6th May 1968.

Immediately to the south west of here was the next passenger station, Junction

37

Tottenham & Hampstead Joint Committee
(L.N.E.R. and L M S)

CLOSING OF
JUNCTION ROAD
AND
HORNSEY ROAD
STATIONS

The London and North Eastern and London Midland and Scottish Railways hereby give notice that on and from Monday, 3rd May, 1943, Junction Road and Hornsey Road Stations **WILL BE CLOSED**

For passenger travel and parcels traffic, the alternative Stations are :—

JUNCTION ROAD—KENTISH TOWN or UPPER HOLLOWAY
HORNSEY ROAD—CROUCH HILL or UPPER HOLLOWAY

April, 1943. C.LA 2. E.R.O. 53330 1.

Closure Notice for Hornsey Road and Junction Road stations.
D. Brennand Collection

Road.

Junction Road, or *Junction Road for Tufnell Park* to give it its full title, stood on the east side of its namesake, and consisted of two platforms with wooden buildings.

It was opened on 1st January 1872, and was no doubt very busy in its heyday. However the seeds for its destruction were sown early in the present century with the opening of the nearby Charing Cross, Euston & Hampstead Railway station at Tufnell Park in 1907, together with competition from local tramways. Not surprisingly, passengers drifted away from the somewhat grubby steam trains, and transferred their allegiance to Mr. Yerkes' smart new 'Electric Tube' just up the road.

Junction Road nevertheless remained open despite its falling patronage, although by the 1930's it seems to have been little used at all. In a 1937 poem, John Betjeman described it as *"a lonely station"* with a single gaslight to illuminate the booking hall.

With various restraints brought on by wartime conditions it became a prime candidate for closure, and passenger services were finally withdrawn on 3rd May 1943, the same day as Hornsey Road.

The buildings survived into the postwar period, but succumbed sometime in the 1950's. A photograph taken in 1951 shows them as still more or less intact, albeit rather tatty.

Rather surprisingly, the street which runs parallel with the south side of the site still retains the name 'Station Road", although nothing now remains of the station itself.

Unfortunately the same can also be said of the nearby signal box which once boasted the rather odd, if appropriate name, of Junction Road Junction. It was constructed in 1883, and controlled the section of line where the THJ route to Gospel Oak parted company with the Midland tracks to Kentish Town and Haverstock Hill.

Following the introduction of a new pre-fabricated panel box south of Upper Holloway, the structure at Junction Road Junction was rendered redundant, and therefore closed in November 1985. The 102 year old brick and timber building survived for a short while, but was eventually demolished following fire damage. At the time of closure it was the oldest surviving Midland Railway signalbox in the country.

For many years, the local passenger service on the line had operated between Barking and Kentish Town, but since 5th January 1981, these trains have used Gospel Oak as their western terminus instead. Following this diversion, the north to east section of the Kentish Town triangle, between Mortimer Street Junction and Engine Shed Junction, was closed completely and subsequently lifted.

Resuming our journey, the Midland route diverges on the up side and descends towards Highgate Road low level, whilst we continue to Gospel Oak.

Above: Junction Road station looking east in the early years of the present century. The nameboard above the entrance to the GER Tufnell Park goods depot can just be seen behind the platform building on the right.

Lens of Sutton

Below: Junction Road station, derelict and forlorn. c1951.

Author's Collection

40

The former High level station had its entrance beneath the railway bridge on the west side of Highgate Road. This consisted of a simple arched doorway through which access was made to the booking office. It was opened on 21st July 1868, temporarily closed along with the other original stations on the line early in 1870, then finally abandoned on 1st October 1915. A 25" OS plan published that year clearly shows the premises, and indicates that the buildings were all situated near the Gospel Oak end, whilst the platforms themselves extended eastwards above the main road. Unfortunately photographs appear to be almost totally non-existent, so it would be impossible to try and describe the structure.

The doorway at street level still survives, but now leads into a workshop. The old gaslamp bracket which once surmounted it also remained for many years, but this has now been removed. The former platform site is just about discernable, although nothing of any real substance still exists.

A commercial postcard view of Highgate Road, looking towards Kentish Town in the first decade of the 20th Century. The entrance to the High Level station can be seen beneath the bridge on the right hand side, and just beyond this is the street level building of the Low Level. This is the only photograph known to the author which shows anything of these two stations whilst still in use and intact.

Alan A. Jackson Collection

The same can also be said of the short lived Midland station of Highgate Road Low Level, which only functioned between 17th December 1900, and 1st March 1918. This was sited deep in cutting, and also had its entrance to the west of the main road. There are marks on the adjoining walls which indicate a former stairway, but other than these everything had vanished. Again, the station doesn't seem to have been photographed.

A Kentish Town - Barking train passes the site of Highgate Road Low Level station
on Saturday January 3rd, 1981, the last day of operation
before the service was diverted to Gospel Oak.

J.E. Connor

Just west of the erstwhile High Level station, another curve diverged to the south. This also led round to Kentish Town, and was opened by the Midland Railway on 3rd January 1870.

After passing the site of some sidings, our train crosses above Gordon House Road and draws to a stand at Gospel Oak station, which adjoins the North London Line premises of the same name. This is, and always has been, a single platform affair, although the alignment was altered slightly before its 1981 restoration to allow for the provision of an extra track.

During the initial building of the line, a station was partially constructed here, and work was started on a locomotive turntable. However, the Company ran out of

Above: The abandoned THJR station at Gospel Oak,
viewed from the brakevan of a cross-London freight in 1968.

J.E. Connor

Below: First day at the new Gospel Oak platform, 5th January 1981.

I. Baker

money by June 1868, and both projects were abandoned before completion. The unfinished station was dismantled in 1870, and the turntable well later filled in.

The line was finally completed with financial backing from the Midland, and Gospel Oak station eventually opened on 4th June 1888.

However, fierce opposition from both the North London and London North Western Railways resulted in the THJR line not being physically connected with their own route, as they feared this would provide a rival link to the east London docks. This remained the case until 1916 when a junction was finally installed. However, four years after, this was taken out of use, and promptly lifted.

The THJR station retained its regular passenger service until 6th September 1926, after which only special trains continued to operate during summer bank holidays until 7th August 1939.

The brick station building was soon demolished leaving just the grass grown platform still in-situ.

The junction was restored from 11th March 1940, and the connection continues to provided a valuable link for cross London freight workings.

The LNWR signalbox at the junction remained in use until late 1984, when it was destroyed by a fire which also resulted in the death of the signalman. Following this, a temporary structure was erected on the station platform, but this was soon replaced by a permanent new panel box, similar in appearance to the one at Upper Holloway.

Having arrived at Gospel Oak we have to take our leave of the train which has carried us on our twelve and a quarter mile journey from Barking. A journey on which we have rumbled on viaduct above east end streets, viewed the complexity of lines around South Tottenham, and travelled through the leafy cuttings of North London suburbia. To some it might not represent one of the country's greatest rail journeys, but for those with a love of London it's certainly one of the most fascinating.

Tottenham & Forest Gate Joint Committee.
This Ticket is issued subject to the Regulations &
conditions stated in the Co's Time Tables & Bills.
THIRD CLASS.   THIRD CLASS.
AVAILABLE ON DAY OF ISSUE ONLY.
BLACK HORSE ROAD to
WALTHAMSTOW
FARE 1d.   FARE 1d.

MIDLAND RAILWAY. This Ticket is issued
subject to the Regulations & Conditions stated in
the Company's Time Tables & Bills.
THIRD CLASS.   THIRD CLASS.
AVAILABLE ON DAY OF ISSUE ONLY.
South Tottenham & Stamford Hill to
EAST HAM (L.T.S.)
FARE 6d.   FARE 6d.

TOTTENHAM & HAMPSTEAD JOINT RY
NOT TRANSFERABLE. This ticket is issued
subject to the General Notices, Regulations
and Conditions in the Company's current Time
Tables, Book of Regulations and Bills.
Available for three days, including day of issue
SOUTH TOTTENHAM to
JUNCTION ROAD
Fare / s \ 6d.
THIRD / 1395 \ CLASS
JUNCTION RD

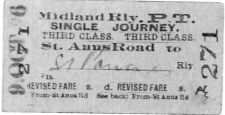

Midland Rly. P.T.
SINGLE JOURNEY.
THIRD CLASS. THIRD CLASS.
St. Anns Road to
Rly.
REVISED FARE s. d. REVISED FARE s.
From St Anns Rd See back) From St Anns Rd

TOTTENHAM & HAMPSTEAD JOINT RY
NOT TRANSFERABLE. This ticket is issued
subject to the General Notices, Regulations
and Conditions in the Company's current Time
Tables, Book of Regulations and Bills.
Available for 3 days, including day of issue.
HARRINGAY PARK to
ST ANN'S ROAD
Fare / s \ 1½d
THIRD / 1391 \ CLASS
ST ANN'S RD

T. & H. Junct. Rly. - Mid. & G. E. Joint Comm.
This Ticket is issued subject to the Regulations &
conditions stated in the Co's Time Tables & Bills.
THIRD CLASS.   THIRD CLASS
AVAILABLE ON DAY OF ISSUE ONLY.
CROUCH HILL to
HIGHGATE ROAD (for Parlia-
ment Hill)
FARE 1½d.   FARE 1½d.
CrouchH HighgateR CrouchH HighgateR

MIDLAND RAILWAY. This Ticket is
issued subject to the Regulations & Conditions
stated in the Company's Time Tables & Bills.
THIRD CLASS.   THIRD CLASS.
Hornsey Road to
GOWER STREET (MET)
Change at King's ✠ (Met.)
FARE 4½d.   FARE 4½d.
Hornsey Rd Gower St Hornsey Rd Gower St

T. & H. Junct. Rly. - Mid. & G. E. Joint Comm.
This Ticket is issued subject to the Regulations &
conditions stated in the Co's Time Tables & Bills.
THIRD CLASS.   THIRD CLASS.
AVAILABLE ON DAY OF ISSUE ONLY.
Upper Holloway to
HIGHGATE ROAD
(FOR PARLIAMENT HILL)
FARE 1d.   FARE 1d.
U. Holloway HighgateRd U. Holloway HighgateRd

A selection of Tickets

J.E. Connor

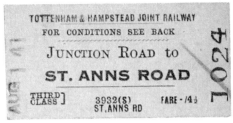

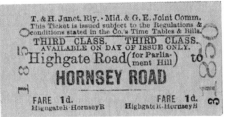

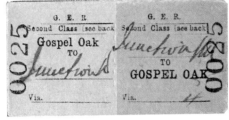

A selection of Tickets

J.E. Connor

PASSENGER STATION OPENINGS AND CLOSURES

	OPENED	CLOSED	NOTES
Barking	13.4.1854 *(L.T.& S.R.)*		
Black Horse Road	9.7.1894 *(T.& F.G.R.)*	14.12.1981 *(B.R.)*	
Blackhorse Road	14.12.1981 *(B.R.)*		
Crouch Hill	21.7.1868 *(T.& H.J.R)*		(1)
East Ham	31.3.1858 *(L.T.& S.R)*		(2)
Gospel Oak	4.6.1888 *(T.& H.J.R.)*	6.9.1926 *(T.&H.J.R)*	(3)
Gospel Oak	5.1.1981 *(B.R.)*		
Green Lanes	1.6.1880 *(T.&H.J.R)*		(4)
Highgate Road High Level	21.7.1868 *(T.&H.J.R.)*	1.10.1915 *(T.&H.J.R)*	(1)
Highgate Road Low Level	17.12.1900 *(Midland)*	1.3.1918 *(Midland)*	
Hornsey Road	1.1.1872 *(T&H.J.R)*	3.5.1943 *(T.&H.J.R)*	
Junction Road *for Tufnell Park*	1.1.1872 *(T&H.J.R)*	3.5.1943 *(T.&H.J.R)*	
Kentish Town	13.7.1868 *(Midland)*		(5)
Leyton	9.7.1894 *(T.&F.G.R.)*		(6)
Leytonstone	9.7.1894 *(T.&F.G.R.)*		(7)
St Ann's Road	2.10.1882 *(T.& H.J.R)*	9.8.1942 *(T.&H.J.R)*	
South Tottenham & Stamford Hill	1.5.1871 *(T.&H.J.R)*		(8)
Upper Holloway	21.7.1868 *(T.&H.J.R)*		(1)
Walthamstow	9.7.1894 *(T.&F.G.R)*		(9)
Wanstead Park	9.7.1894 *(T.&F.G.R)*		
Woodgrange Park	9.7.1894 *(L.T.& S.R)*		

NOTES

(1) Temporarily closed 31.1.1870 - 1.10.1870

(2) Kentish Town services withdrawn 15.9.1958

(3) Partially constructed 1868, but abandoned before completion due to financial problems. Unfinished station demolished 1870. New single platform adjoining L & N.W.R. (Hampstead Junction) station of same name on date shown above. closed to regular passenger traffic in 1926, but continued to be used during summer bank holidays until 7.8.1939.

(4) Renamed Harringay Park, Green Lanes 1883., Harringay Park 18.6.1951, Harringay Stadium 27.10.1958, Harringay East 12.5.1990, and Harringay Green Lanes 8.7.1991.

(5) Barking services withdrawn 5.1.1981, and re-routed to serve Gospel Oak.

(6) Renamed Leyton. Midland Road 1.5.1949

(7) Renamed Leytonstone, High Road 1.5.1949

(8) Suffix *'And Stamford Hill'* dropped 1949

(9) Renamed Walthamstow Queens Road 6.5.1968.

APPENDIX TWO
GOODS DEPOT OPENINGS AND CLOSURES.

	OPENED	CLOSED	NOTES
Black Horse Road	1.9.1894 *(T.& F.G.R.)*	7.12.1964 *(B.R.)*	
Green Lanes	1.6.1880 *(T.& H.J.R)*	3.2.1964 *(B.R.)*	(1)
Leyton	1.9.1894 *(T.& F.G.R.)*	6.5.1968 *(B.R.)*	(1)
Leytonstone	1.9.1894 *(T.& F.G.R.)*	6.5.1968 *(B.R.)*	(1)
South Tottenham & Stamford Hill	1.5.1871 *(Midland)*	4.7.1966 *(B.R.)*	(1)
Tufnell Park	15.2.1886 *(G.E.R.)*	6.5.1968 *(B.R.)*	
Upper Holloway	c1870 *(Midland)*	6.5.1968 *(B.R.)*	
Walthamstow Queens Road	1.9.1894 *(T.& F.G.R.)*	6.5.1968 *(B.R.)*	
Woodgrange Park	c 9.1894 *(L.T.& S.R.)*	7.12.1964 *(B.R.)*	

NOTE
(1) Subject to same renamings as adjoining passenger stations

KEY TO RAILWAY COMPANY INITIALS USED IN APPENDICES

B.R.	British Rail
G.E.R.	Great Eastern Railway
L.T. & S.R.	London Tilbury & Southend Railway
T. & F.G.R.	Tottenham & Forest Gate Railway
T.& H.J.R.	Tottenham & Hampstead Junction Railway
	(later Tottenham & Hampstead Joint Railway)